FLOWERS OF THE WEST INDIES

FLOWERS OF THE WEST INDIES with 32
pages of full color photographs

Exotic colors in flowers you'll see here, colors planted and grown in the riotous garden
of history, for many nations contributed to
the plants and flowers of the Caribbean and
Bahamas . . . some cultivated with loving
hands . . . some plundered with bloody
hands . . . mixed and splashed colors.

Perfumed witchery by moonlight and by
sunlight . . . flashing floral color against
stained-glass blue skies or green tapestries,
tropical flowers enhance chameleon-like
changes of scenery catching the imagination
of all who see these islands. The sunshine
vastness of playful flower-brightened coasts
changes inland to flower, fern and moss
draped ancient trees with orchids and bro-
meliads on their branches. "Flowers of the
West Indies" captures this loveliness . . .
helps you get the most out of these sights
and scents.

HANS W. HANNAU
   Photography and design

JEANNE GARRARD
   Story

FLOWERS of the WEST INDIES

ARGOS INC.
MIAMI

Library of Congress Catalog Card Number 74-101410

D.L.B-33.691 - 74

FLOWERS OF THE WEST INDIES

Magically conjuring up tantalizing fragrances...sights...adventures of pirates and plant explorers...sounds...feelings...passions..:entrancing potpourri—enough to dazzle your senses—"Flowers of the West Indies" is a bright new name. One you'll long treasure!

Names such as Musaceae, Saccharum officinarum, Ananas comosus and Vanilla fragrans certainly are not as famous as Columbus, Admiral Nelson, Captain Morgan, Bluebeard and Bligh...but these strange names had as much—or even more—to do with creating today's West Indies.

You know these strange scientific names—no doubt—by their common names for plants (bananas, sugar cane, pineapple and vanilla) but you may not know they've changed history even more than well known names.

WHEN YOU DISCOVER THESE FLOWER ISLANDS

Wild and cultivated beauty often overcomes today's visitors on their first tropical vacations to the West Indies.

Bombarding their senses are colorful kaleidoscopes of flowers and flowering trees exploding like flames from green jungle mazes or tropical forests sliced open by cascading rivers tumbling down to rocky seascapes or white (and black) sand beaches surrounded by azure lagoons or reef smashing waves.

Psychedelic flashes of changing scenes and changing flowering plants from island to island are immediately exciting and confusing to the uninitiated visitor. The Caribbean changed one visitor into a plant-lover. "I **had** to learn about one flower or doubt my sight," she explained. Arising early, she looked out on the Caribbean landscape and particularly admired a large, pure white flowering bush right by her window. Returning after shopping, a glance up to the window-view made her grab up her packages. She thought she was in the wrong room...for the bush outside **this** window was covered, not with white but with showy **rose-pink** flowers! Her room number and key matched. She decided she'd been mistaken about the flower color that morning. Surprise took over late that afternoon. She returned to dress for dinner. She couldn't believe her eyes.

The bush outside her window had changed again. Now it had dull RED Blossoms!

Mysterious? Not in the tropics. She just met her first Hibiscus Mutabilis—the Changeable Rose. Like so many of the unusual tropical flowers and chameleon-like trees, this lovely flower changes color all during the day—magically changing from pure white in early morning to delicate rose-pink by noon, then to a deeper and deeper pink all afternoon, ending with a dull red just before it closes in the evening. Surprise turned into fascinated amazement for this visitor. The more she learned about this Hibiscus and its family, the more unbelievable nature in the tropics became.

Fascinating additional facts she learned about Hibiscus while admiring all the single and double types; gay and gaudy colors from flaming red and deep crimsons to sun yellows and virgin whites (some with a center or eye of a different color):

perfume musk (much used in European perfume) comes from yellow Hibiscus, (H. abelmoschus); **okra** (vegetable food) is a seed pod of yellow with red center Hibiscus (H. esculentus); **hemp fibre** is made from yellowish with dark purple center Hibiscus stems (H. cannabinus); **sweet drinks, jams and jellies** are made from red and rose mix Hibiscus sepals, (H. sabdariffa); **acid** is extracted from immature calyx and bracts of red and rose mixed Hibiscus, (H. Roselle); **bootblacks** of tropics use red Hibiscus flowers to polish shoes, (H. rosa-sinensis); **whips** are made from another Hibiscus fibre, (*H. arborea*); **hedges and wind breaks** on cacao plantations are often common red Hibiscus. *(H. rosa-sinensis)*; **various species** of Hibiscus come from such diverse places as East Indies, West Indies, Australia, Asia, Africa, China, Japan, Hawaii, all Tropics in fact, and Central American countries; over 200 known species of herbs, shrubs and trees are Hibiscus; most commonly, Hibiscus and its hybrids are planted for ornamental purposes because of their large colorful blossoms.

Oddities of the plant world found in the West Indies constantly confounded her for Hibiscus are the commonest yet perhaps the **least** of its colorfully interesting flowers.

"I saw long tassels of reddish-purple flowers on drooping finger-thick stems, too," she said. "They looked exactly as if they'd come off my Chenille bedspread." (Chenille Plant—*Acalypha hispida*). She wasn't alone in amazement. (These are also called "Red Hot Cat-Tails").

A Mid-western hobby gardener told me of his experiences on his first Caribbean trip. "Why I saw Shrimps on bushes!" He acted like I wouldn't believe him but went on exclaiming his "finds." "And I saw Shaving Brushes on Trees! *(Bombax ellipticum* or *Callistemon lanceolatus).* I spotted fire in a tree top but it turned out to be a mirage caused by the Flamboyant or Royal Poinciana tree" (a common sight in summer and fall). "Some botanist tried to confuse me by saying this was not a true Poinciana. Then he said it wasn't native but had been brought there from Madagascar. Of course, he may be right. I saw coffee plants all over these islands. Coffee is an Egyptian plant...made Brazil rich...and the Brazilian Rubber grows best in Malaya and a Mexican Rose we saw near that Poinciana, looks exactly like one of my Hydrangeas but comes from Madagascar...so it could be true...but how in the world could all these foreign plants do so well here and—most important—how did they all get here?"

International bouquets of flowers from all parts of the world growing so beautifully in the West Indies are easily enjoyed without prior knowledge of the region and its history...but unraveling mysteries is fun.

EXPLOSIONS—PEOPLE & NATURE—RAKE SOIL

Masters of deceit...pirates...explorers...plunderers...plant lovers...conquistadors ...zealous missionaries...plantation owners...slaves...slavers—all splashed vivid pigments into this seething cauldron of colors before it became a garden. But it began to boil before that...

Volcanoes illustrate this transformation (of metaphor as well as physical properties) from boiling cauldron to growing garden—their molten masses bubble and explode. Then they erupt, casting out lava, cinders and ash which finally cools and supplies nourishment to its sides that plants may bloom upon its slopes. Before the modern Caribbean Islands of today could bloom as they do, centuries of turmoil and growth had to mature.

7,000 ISLANDS PLANTED

The "Master Designer" placed these 7,000-odd islands and reefs in the most strategic "growing" location on earth.

Further blessing these tropical islands, the "Master Designer" added "Trade Winds." Trade Winds gave these tropics their greatest natural advantage.

Centuries of trade winds drifted seeds across the Atlantic Ocean where frothing waves tossed them on tropic shores. These trade winds blow from an easterly direction most of the year. They bring moisture from sea-evaporation into clouds across these islands. Clouds get blown inland, spilling some water in showers. Light showers become rain when trade winds blow clouds inland to the mountains. The winds curve upward to flow over the tops. As they curve upward, cooler mountain air causes condensation of moisture in the rain clouds which overflow giving the tropics almost daily life-giving drenches of fresh water. Some rain forests have more than 200-300 inches of rainfall each year. Rich topsoil washed down into valleys and plains building layers of fertile soil through the centuries.

Foreign seeds sprang to life. Birds and insects—some blown by trade winds and hurricanes—followed seeds to fertilize plants and pollinate flowers...creating ever larger numbers of plants and flowers.

ISLAND INDIANS DIG OUT FOOD

Man appeared in the West Indies...

First, as Indians (we know not whether placed there by the "Master Designer" or from other lands or both).

Primitive Indians lived by eating wild roots, fish and fruits. Coconuts furnished food, water, milk, sugar, oil, liquor, fuel, wood for boats and thatch for homes (origin of the coconut is still disputed but whether from Old World or New, it was important to natives). Supple jack or Paullinia was (and is) used as a fish poison to make catching easier.

Indians of higher intellect than the primitives—such as Arawaks, Aztecs, Mayas and Incas—cultivated and improved their plants much as we do today (The Vatican Library in Rome shows a record of the use of plants in medicine translated from "An Aztec Herbal of 1552"). Some historians believe these New World Indians are descendants of the ancient Egyptians. It is interesting to note that Egyptian priests had medicines and that the Papyri mention certain medicinal plants in use at that time—aloe, acacia and cassia—that are found in the Caribbean.

Certainly some of the plants early New World Indians cultivated such as the pumpkin, corn, potato, yam, tomato, squash, peanut, pineapple and bean, have spread all over the world. Pharmaceutical drugs still of importance today—cocaine and quinine—were used by Peruvian Indians before their conquest by the Spanish. Our records of the West Indians' plant exchange is almost nil but something like the Peruvian coca leaves to chew enabled the Caribs to fight for incredible periods without rest or food...as invaders learned.

ACCIDENTS GRAFT FOREIGN TWIGS

Next, on the human scene, came a Spanish treasure-seeking explorer—Columbus.

Adventure—a dream plus greed—sped these three little ships on their way to find a short route to the back door of Marco Polo's rich spice-land of India, China and the East Indies. An accident thus caused these Islands to be discovered. Enthusiasm—laced with ignorance—caused Columbus to name them the West Indies. He believed he had reached India by sailing west, so he bestowed this misnomer which clings through history and present days.

Another accident—the loss of men and a ship—caused Columbus to "plant" the first group of white men on Hispaniola while he sailed back to spread the glories and beauties of this tropical heaven—and—talk Queen Isabella into financing a second expedition of 17 ships and over 12,000 men with plants to "plant Spanish colonies."

Columbus had discovered—on his first voyage—the peaceful, friendly Arawak Indians and the fierce fighting Caribs. From the Arawaks, he learned about tobacco, cultivating yucca for rum, palms for sweets and how to change the poisonous cassava plant into cassava bread, Indian corn and yams for food and cotton for clothing and hammocks. From the other Indian tribe, the Caribs, he learned more about death-to-invaders when these Indians fought to protect their homelands. It's frightening but interesting to note that the peaceful Arawaks were almost exterminated by white invaders while the Caribs reversed this...but are remembered on maps today because the Caribbean was named for them.

Fleets of Spanish, Portuguese, French, English and Dutch ships followed Columbus as fast as sails and trade winds could bring them.

You've heard many stories about that first period of Spanish exploration, conquest and colonization; then tales of other Old World countries joining in the battle for control of the "Mediterranean of the New World." Actually, Columbus did not find a "New World." He discovered another "Old World" and established "new outposts" such as Santo Domingo with his brother in 1496.

WEEDS BATTLE FLOWERS

From this—the oldest permanent Caucasian settlement in the Americas—were sown gentle botanical seeds and violent biological seeds that sprouted over islands of the Caribbean Sea and surrounding lands.

Good and bad seeds were sown as if broadcast on the winds—as indeed they were.

Flowers and weeds (in all senses of the words in plant world and human world) came from the Santo Domingo port. You may not have heard before of the different types of seeds and plants Columbus brought from Europe and the Canary Islands; that Hernando Cortes, in one of his first letters to his King, asked that no vessel be permitted to sail for New Spain without cereals and other seeds; of how Bernal Diaz Del Castillo planted the first orange trees near Coatzacoalcos; or that De la Vegas sent glowing reports of the celebration when the first grapes from Spain bore fruit at Cuzco.

CROPS SPROUT

Spanish wines were not the only products from colonies and missionaries. Spanish missionaries knew their missions must send products back to Spain but must also be self-sustaining. So, wherever they went, they planted vegetables, fruits, medicinal herbs and flowers to decorate the altars or make garlands for priests to wear on holy days. Each monk or priest brought roots, seeds and cuttings to support life around his mission. But Spanish Kings and Captains were more interested in gold and conquests in the Spanish Main.

OFFSHOOTS OF SLAVERS

Ships which brought slaves did occasionally bring the plants which they were used to eating and with which they could be fed. Just such a fortunate thing happened with the ackee. The first Jamaican botanist, Dr. Clarke, bought the first tiny ackee slips from the captain of a slaver. Dr. Clarke nursed these trees along so well that the ackee is one of Jamaica's most unusual but characteristic dishes of today.

Curiously enough, the ackee—like the cassava Columbus found with the original Indians—is poisonous so it could kill as well as feed slaves. Both require knowledge to use—the cassava must be prepared by boiling off poison; the ackee is non-poisonous **only** when perfectly ripe.

The mango, an Asiatic tree that now grows in all tropics and is, in fact, called the "apple of the tropics," was a staple of slave days. Even today you can see endless lines of mango trees in Central Africa which were planted or thrown away by Arab traders along their slave caravan routes to the sea. The French Government sent the first mango trees from Mauritius to the French West Indies islands in

1782. This ship was captured by an English frigate, *HMS Flora* and Captain Marshall, whose commanding officer, Admiral Lord Rodney, saw their value. Admiral Rodney sent the captured plants to Jamaica to be propagated. They flourished and spread throughout the Caribbean. It's said, no other single plant became more important to the starving poor during the summer.

SPADE-WORK BY BOTANISTS & SAILORS

Breadfruit trees grew wild in Tahiti and other islands of the South Seas. Since the climate of the West Indies was not very different from that of the South Seas, it was thought that breadfruit trees there should be brought to British Caribbean islands for the slaves' food. William Bligh had been Captain Cook's lieutenant on that breadfruit-discovery-voyage so in 1787 *H.M.S. Bounty* was sent under Bligh's command to Tahiti to collect breadfruit and other plants.

The infamous mutiny aboard the *Bounty* kept Bligh from bringing a load of breadfruit to the West Indies but he was sent again in command of *H.M.S. Providence.* On this trip, Bligh brought a cargo of plants which included 352 breadfruit trees which were planted in English Botanical Gardens at Bath and St. Thomas in Jamaica; St. Vincent and later other islands. Today, in fact, you can see a breadfruit tree grown from seed Bligh brought from Tahiti in Kingstown's Botanical Gardens on St. Vincent. However, almost two centuries ago, it was the Jamaican Assembly which bestowed great recognition on Bligh for his services.

BLOOMING OF BOTANICAL GARDENS

Founding of numerous Botanical Gardens in the British West Indies around this same time (the oldest Botanical Garden is known to be over 200 years old and is on St. Vincent Island…Sir Hans Sloane made the British West Indies, especially Jamaica, well known to science during his lifetime—1660-1753) shows the economic value placed upon introducing cheap starch-food for field labor as well as England's interest in botany and gardening.

(Continued on page 33)

CHINESE HIBISCUS
(Hibiscus rosa-sinens

BROMELIAD
AIR PLANT
(*Billbergia
pyramidalis*)

14

PEACH ANGELS TRUMPET
(Datura suaveolens)

DWARF POINCIANA
(Poinciana pulcherrima)

15

PINK POUI TREE *(Tabebuia pentaphylla)*

**SKY VINE
THUMBERGIA**
*(Thumbergia
grandiflora)*

CERIMAN
(Monstera
deliciosa

The fruit is
delicious
Edible

Also
It is in Botanical Garden - Swash. DC

CANDLE
BUSH
(Cassia alata)

← RED BOTTLE
BRUSH TREE
(*Callistemon
lanceolatus*)

→ YELLOW ELDER
(*Tecoma stans*)

MORNING GLORY-BUSH ↑
(Ipomea carnea)

FLAME OF THE FOREST, AFRICAN →
TULIP TREE *(Spathodea campanulat*

←
ANTHURIUM
(Anthurium andraeanum)

→
ALOE
HEALING PLANT
(Aloe vera)

25

CAPE
MYRTLE
(Lagerstroemia
speciosa)

GOLDEN
SHOWER
(Cassia
fistula)

27

Description of foregoing pictures

RED GINGER, FIRE GINGER, FIERY FEATHER (*Alpinia purpurata*)
Cover

Large open-spaced rich crimson bracts as delicate as petals hide shy true flowers. This flaming spike stands erect and proud of its rosy-crimson beauty against dark green blade-shaped leaves. As the flower matures, it elongates and tiny green plantlets pop out between the bracts. As they grow and add weight to the feather end long stalk, the head bends over. Reaching ground, the plantlets take root and grow. Ginger comes in many other colors and shapes.

CHINESE HIBISCUS, GARDEN RED HIBISCUS (*Hibiscus rosa-sinensis*)
page 13

"Leading lady" all over the West Indian Islands is the Hibiscus whose native country is not definitely known but is credited to China or Japan. Red is probably the commonest color but yellow is almost equally popular. Recently, a white and green variegated leaf variety has become popular from the original stock plant in Trinidad's Royal Botanic Gardens; it flourishes all through the islands. Most flowers are a showy 4½ or 5 inches in diameter. There are double varieties too.

BROMELIAD, PRETTY PINEAPPLE, AIR PLANT (*Billbergia pyramidalis*)
page 14

This charming member of the Pineapple family spreads easily but retains individual broad-leafed open rosettes of green-gold shade. Its short erect flower spike builds up to a large compact head of radiant pink bracts and masses of pink flowers tipped in brilliant blue. Of the 40 genera and 1,000 species, many are grown on the ground or in trees for their showy flowers or brightly colored foliage.

PEACH ANGELS TRUMPET (*Datura suaveolens*)
page 15

Pale salmon colored trumpet flowers 10-12 inches long hang from a shrub, 8 to 15 ft. high, wafting a musk-like perfume in twilight and evening hours.

DWARF POINCIANA (*Poinciana pulcherrima*)

Often called Flame Poinciana or Pride of Barbados, it grows all over the Tropical Americas and its exact origin is still being debated. The feathery compound leaves are deciduous on the 12 to 15 ft. rather thorny shrub but the flashing red or yellow flowers appear practically all year long.

RAY ORCHIDS, MOTH ORCHIDS
ritaenopsis Dorette)

PINK POUI TREE, PINK TRUMPET,
PINK TECOMA, APAMATA, TABEBUIA
(Tabebuia pentaphylla or Tecoma
pentaphylla)
page 16

Giant bouquet of pinkish-rose petunia-like trumpets cover this West Indies native. It blooms when only 3 feet tall on up to when it is a 60 foot tree.

SKY VINE (Thumbergia grandiflora)
page 17

Large blue flaring flowers with yellow throats and deep green leaves are from India, but now growing all over the Caribbean, Bahamas and southern Florida.

CANDLEBUSH, GOLDEN CANDLE,
ACAPULCO, CANDLESTICK SENNA
(Cassia alata)   page 18

Named, of course, because its inflorescences begin as erect spikes of candle-like clusters of bright yellow buds on curved candelabra-like stems. Flowers open from the base upward over a period of several weeks. It can attain a height of 8 feet and is truly striking when tight buds keep the cylindrical shape or open into fluffy "suns." It is grown on most of the islands for it can even stand arid drought areas found on some islands. Below one branch is a painted leaf Croton, another commonly grown shrub.

MONSTERA DELICIOSA
(Monstera deliciosa)
page 19

Monstera Deliciosas are also called 'Ceriman' or "Giant Jack in the Pulpit." About 21 species are also called "Swiss Cheese" plants. They are from Mexico and Guatemala primarily but grow well in the West Indies. This plant is known as Philodendron pertusum in its juvenile stage. The Monstera Deliciosa's unique calla-like "flower" has a heavy-textured curled spathe, that is hood-like pointed, as an up-ended boat, protecting a cone-like or rocket-shaped bisexual spadix with divided six-sided corn-like fruit sections. It takes about 14 months to ripen, and the entire fruit has a slight pineapple aroma.

RED BOTTLE BRUSH TREE
(Callistemon lanceolatus)
page 20

Weeping willow type branches of this tree are adorned with bristly cylindrical spikes 2-4" long of red flowers that look exactly like brushes used to clean baby bottles—except that they are scarlet. Odd inflorescences are composed of separated spikes of red flowers with numerous dominant red stamens sticking out all around the stem. Usually a small tree, it may grow to 25 feet with long, narrow greyish green leaves.

YELLOW ELDER, CHRISTMAS HOPE
(Tecoma stans)
page 21

Funnel-shaped yellow clusters appear on this native shrub or small tree—especially on drier coasts, but found all over the islands. Flat pods hang down and contain winged seed. The showy yellow flowers stand out against feather-fashioned leaflets. It is the National Flower of the Bahamas.

POTATO BUSH, POTATO TREE, MORNING GLORY-BUSH
(Ipomea carnea)
page 22

Large showy trumpet-shaped flowers are rather flimsy in the wind but delicate mauvish-pink petals flow into deeper colors within the throat and can be enjoyed all day. This perennial, with its trailing or bushy habit, is a Tropical American native found abundantly over the countryside and in village gardens. It is so common and so commonly called Potato Bush or Potato Tree that few people know its botanical name.

AFRICAN TULIP TREE, FLAME OF THE FOREST *(Spathodea campanulata)*
page 23

A striking West African forest tree of very rapid growth has become prolific in the West Indies. Scarlet bell flowers pop from claw-shaped buds. These buds give the tree another name—Fountain Tree—for they hold compressed water which spurts forth when small boys use them as water pistols or when a bird happens to pierce one with his beak. These large red blossoms flicker in the treetops, thrilling birds and visitors.

ANTHURIUM, FLAMINGO FLOWER, HEART FLOWER *(Anthurium andraeanum)*
page 24

Heart-shaped patent-leather like and brilliant red of this flower is its spathe. True flowers are tiny and crowded in the dense spike or spadix. Here, pictured in one of Martinique's rain forests, are dozens of buds—such as the tightly curled one just below the two open hearts—showing as flashes of red against the green heart-shaped leaves. The Anthurium genus is widely grown for its fine foliage or its striking flower spathe. A sister plant *(A. scherzerianum)* is also called the Flamingo Flower or Pig Tail Flower. Although its spathe is colored like these pictures, its spadix coils like a small corkscrew and the spathe is never quite as waxy or brilliant red, orange-red (or even as white) as the one pictured here. Nor does its bloom last as long. This Anthurium flower will last for the florist as a cut-flower for three weeks when cut at its prime. It will last even longer on the plant.

ALOE, HEALING PLANT, SHOOT OF PARADISE
(Aloe vera or Aloe Barbadensis)
page 25

Aloes are mostly South African. Probably the first ones brought to the New World were smuggled by slaves and slavers because of the healing powers of the leaves. Aloe is mentioned as a cleansing medicine in the Bible and Egyptian papyri of 1600 B.C. Legend says Aloe was the only plant Adam and Eve brought from the Garden of Eden—giving it another common name, Shoot of Paradise. There are 100 species but only a few are popular. Flowers hang in clusters of bell-shapes in red or yellow depending on the type. It's hard to believe but these succulent plants are members of the Lily family. Medicinal properties of the leaves are today used in modern medicine and beauty preparations but have been used for centuries as "instant" burn cure, pain reliever, tonic and laxative.

GOLDEN SHOWER, SHOWER OF GOLD, CASSIA *(Cassia fistula)*
page 26

Golden Shower shrubs or trees have large clusters of bright yellow blossoms which seem to cascade down the limbs in grape-like bunches. The flowers have five petals with long curving stamens and pistil that stick out from the center of the bloom.

CRAPE MYRTLE, QUEEN OF FLOWERS, QUEEN FLOWER, CRAPE OR FLOWER CRAPE *(Lagerstroemia indica, also L. speciosa, and L. flos-reginae)*
page 27

Tight pink clusters 4 to 9 inches long adorn bushes and trees in this genus in showy masses. Scientists argue the name with *L. speciosa* preferred. Size of the plant decides the botanical name (up to 20 feet tall the Crape Myrtle is known as *L. indica* from China; a tree up to 50 or 60 feet tall is called *L. speciosa* or *L. flos-reginae* from India-Australia areas called Queen's Crape Myrtle but popularly all of these are loved and called Queen Flowers.

SPRAY ORCHIDS, MOTH ORCHIDS
(Doritaenopsis Dorette)
page 28

Orchids of all types bloom in the Caribbean. One of these islands, for example —Jamaica—has over 200 different species native to its forests with 73 of these exclusively native. Species and hybrids from all parts of the world have been brought to all the tropic islands by modern enthusiasts so it is not unusual to find various kinds of orchid blooms in island gardens.

(Continued from Page 12)

ROYALTY COLLECTS FLOWERS

During the reign of William and Mary, for instance, the Queen had three hot-houses. She commissioned many plant collectors to bring back "exoticks." In all lands, as people were no longer forced to grow plants for food and began to accumulate wealth and position, they turned to growing flowers for pleasure.

England—long a leader in sailing ships and horticultural interest—continued to lead the world in plant explorations and introductions for food, medicine and pleasure. The Royal Botanical Gardens at Kew acted as THE medium of horticultural exchange between the tropics of the Old World and the New World. Of course, skilled growers of Holland, Spain and France contributed greatly too, as did the United States, but the English remained the leaders in botany.

FLOWER-POWER OUTGROWS FARMING

As you know from botany, the plant-kingdom is made up in only four main groups with flowering plants as the last great group to appear on earth. So far as plants are concerned, the flowering group became the leaders.

Orchids became the "royalty" with Cattleyas the "Queens." Yet—like the West Indies—Cattleyas were discovered by accident. It is no accident that orchids are grown all over the West Indies today. Today—the world over—there are more flowering plants than all other plants put together. The tropics—especially the West Indies—has become a melting pot of plants and flowers from all parts of the world.

Flowers—large and colorful, tiny or fragrant—produce the lure to insects or birds that pollinate them, making seeds to reproduce and multiply themselves. Man cannot live without flowers and seeds. Man cannot travel in space without flowers (producing food and oxygen for his trip). Perhaps we have learned from the ingenious methods seeds have of immigrating to new fertile homes...certainly flowers make our present homes more enjoyable and these islands in the sun more colorful. The various battles and wars—when certain islands changed hands and governments a number of times between Spanish, French, Dutch and

English—did not change plants and flowers, they merely added to their worldly mixture. In 1900, David Fairchild organized the Office of Foreign Seed and Plant Introduction in the United States Department of Agriculture. It became one of the most important agencies working on an exchange of economic and garden plants between Tropical American countries and other parts of the world. This exchange is still going on today but many of these plant lives started with the immigrants in the West Indies.

FOREIGN FLOWERS IMMIGRATE

Melting pots of the world are made up of immigrants—some immigrate of their own free will; others, have been brought as captives or slaves. Our orchards, vegetable and flower gardens are full of these immigrants too.

The West Indies have been a flower "melting pot." Some flower seeds came by air—hundreds of years before we humans knew how to travel by air—by ships or merely floating on water. Some seeds even hitch-hiked on birds, animals and man...then in turn, man lived on these plants to bring the West Indies into civilized flower as it is today. As men spend less and less time wresting a livelihood from the soil and prosperity grows in these islands, more and more flowers-for-pleasure will bloom on these tropic shores.

GARDEN MICROCOSM

Delightful floral designs of the world—a garden microcosm—serve as artistic settings for flower jewels in the West Indies today that illustrate transplants from other countries.

It's not unusual to see the strictly English "cottage" garden or rock gardens with perennial borders spiced with variety and Victorian profusion of blooms.

Jamaica abounds with flower and plant variety. For instance, there are over 200 different species of orchids (73 peculiar to this island alone) and 500 species of ferns. Jamaica's Hope Botanical Gardens and other British islands (especially such as Barbados, St. Kitts, St. Vincent, Antigua, Tobago and the aromatic spice gardens of Grenada) show the traditional formal English style with different levels built or discovered to take advantage of magnificent views—most often cerulean water or cliffs and clouds. Other areas show Elizabethan, Georgian and Jacobean styles including massive clipped hedges, broad expanses of lawns spiked by Parterre patterns of annuals, bordered by luxurious growing trees. Parterres—those geometric arrangements of ornamental shaped beds separated by a pattern of walks or turf areas—are found in business sections such as downtown Kingston, village greens and in Botanical Gardens as well as private estates. At other times, flowers will be grouped in formal-design gardens flanked by tremendous natural-istic areas left in a semi-wild condition that was so loved by Queen Victoria. (Some visitors, unfortunately, do not appreciate this form of semi-wild garden which may or may not have masses of flowers. They fail to realize it is "planned design" not "undeveloped" land.)

Flowers somehow seem to match the fairy-painted old-world "Londontown village" of Bridgetown in Barbados and the "quaint European village" atmosphere of St. George's in Grenada.

French gardens (such as those to be found in Martinique, Haiti's Kenscoff and Le Cap areas, Guadeloupe and even the French Village in St. Thomas Island) are really minor adaptations of Italian Renaissance—French flavor designs—but more sophisticated, more tropical and more limited to Government or official buildings. French style garden pavilions, treillage and parterre patterns are elaborate scroll designs in more lavish estates with garden sculpture and iron grillwork more fanciful and romantic to accent flowers. Martinique and Guadeloupe grow a great variety of flowers like the waxy Anthuriums (which grow wild and are raised commercially in Martinique and Guadeloupe).

Spanish patio and mission gardens can be seen on many islands—like the Dominican Republic and parts of islands that are no longer controlled by Spain but are Spanish in origin and language (such as Puerto Rico, a U.S. possession).

Trinidad's heterogeneous mixture of races and mingling of cultures reflects in its English Savannah park and architecture of everything from Hindu Temples to Benedictine Monasteries. Its Royal Botanical Gardens at Port-of-Spain reflect the floral beauties of all nations—East Indian, Japanese, French, Spanish, Dutch,

African and local West Indian. All over the island are red flowering immortelles (Erythrina), golden and pink Poui (Tabebuia and Tecoma), lemon grass (Cymbopogen), bamboo, Anthuriums and honey flowers alive with many species of humming birds. Trinidad boasts 27 native genera of orchids including Cattleya *(skinneri)* and the butterfly orchids, Oncidium. Native and introduced orchids are grown naturally or naturalistically on blocks of wood (usually Calabash tree wood). *Vanda teres* has become the commonest orchid in Trinidad while Cattleyas are the most popular genus. Bougainvillea, flame vine and flaming red hibiscus ignite forest greens.

Dutch gardens of the Netherlands Antilles (Curacao, Bonaire, volcanic Saba, Sint Maarten, Sint Eustatius and desert-like Aruba) are as Dutch-pretty and scrubbed-clean as any in Holland—with narrow Dutch-gabled homes, streets and flower charm.

Loveliest old-world Dutch-charm cities are Willemstad in Curacao and Oranjestad in Aruba—both, painted, petted and planted with 17th and 18th century finesse laced with modern civic pride (and perhaps a drop of tourist-drawing eagerness). Striking modern homes and landscaped gardens enhance the suburbs of Willemstad. The Dutch, traditionally, have a masterful way of creating a garden out of wasteland (Holland's submerged land recovered from the sea at least twice; Dutch West Indies islands were all more or less barren and originally not overly wanted by others). Petite gardens in Oranjestad bloom by narrow red-gabled homes. Such flowers as "brides' tears," a pink and white dainty locally called "bruidstranen" shares the spotlight with a pink and white vine called "mannenkarakter." A beautiful modern residential section features more lavish gardens but most homes feature some flowers just as they do in Holland.

Harmonious gardens—each with its own foreign-import flavor—reflect harmonious island living today and a history of growth. After all the fighting and fighting-to-stay-alive, people learn to live as neighbors and intermingle. So, too, do their plants learn to live in new lands until they become a part of it. Thus today we are able (hesitantly) to point to origins of some plants that have become native to the Caribbean Islands or were native in some form before our recorded history.

Much of botanical history was recorded by sea-faring men and missionaries rather than by botanists (although English botanists have worked at taxonomy for over 200 years). So it is inevitable that disagreements will arise about plant origins and common names will confuse blooms—but, happily, these cannot dim our enjoyment of the flowers.

OFFSPRING OF EARLY PLANTS CULTIVATED

Flowers of the West Indies are as colorful, diverse and romantic as the islands themselves.

Plant world families and genera gather here, for there are over 133 families and over 715 genera on a single island. The Palmae family is represented by over 48 genera alone; flowering trees with beautiful (as opposed to tiny) flowers number over 3,000. But for "Flowers of the West Indies," the color will come from the most popular or unusual flowers, vines, flowering shrubs and blooming trees.

The most colorful and most common of these fall into approximately 25 botanical families, with half dozen families leading the way. These families are: the Pea family (Leguminosae), Bignonia family (Bignoniaceae), Spurge or Euphorbia family (Euphorbiaceae), Banana family (Musaceae), Four-O'clock family (Nyctaginaceae), and Pineapple family (Bromeliaceae). Close behind these come the Hibiscus or Mallow family (Malvaceae), Periwinkle or Dogbane family (Apocynaceae), Bellflower family (Campanulaceae) and Cactus family (Cactaceae). Making up the background greens but mostly without showy blooms are Palmae, the Treefern families (Dicksoniaceae & Cyatheaceae) and common ferns (Polypodiaceae & Schizaeaceae).

Interesting and extremely jungle-looking are members of the Ariod family (Araceae with 10 genera or more in the West Indies) whose chief interest to visitors comes from the leaves and luxuriant, growth such as that of Monsteras, Philodendrons and Anthuria (except the showy andraeanum)

Fascinating flowers such as the Passion Flower, Morning Glory family and Ginger family not to mention the Potato and Tomato families and the oddities like insect eating Aristolochias which often look like large swans, pelicans or

Dutchmen's pipes, bloom profusely.

Largest and most important group of garden plants in the world (over 450 genera and estimated 10,000 species) and understandably rating the same in the West Indies, is the Pea Family of herbs, shrubs, trees and vines.

Over 73 genera are popular in the West Indies, some grown for dyes, drugs, oils, gums and timbers but most loved for their spectacular blossoms. Of particular interest are the flaming red and yellow Poincianas; Orchid Trees or Bauhinias (about 150 species) with lavender, white, pink or red blossoms originally from West Indies, China, Africa and India where its bark is valuable in tanning and dyeing while flower buds and leaves are used as vegetables as they are by some Caribbeans, twin leaflets (inseparable pairs) make this easy to remember as the only plant I know named for **two** people—brothers John and Casper Bauhin; Golden, Pink or Rainbow Showers (or cascading Cassias) range from perennial herb size to 30 foot tall trees from India and tropic islands of the Caribbean so often marveled at by vacationers; red Tiger's Claw, Coral Bush or Erythrina are from all tropics and are all red or some hue of red; Powder Puff Bush or Calliandra; and lavender or pink Pea Vine or Canavalia that will grow in wasteland areas.

Perhaps the next most common West Indies family would be the Four-O'clock (since Hibiscus were discussed) with only three genera of flower interest—rare sand verbena, old-fashioned Four-O'clocks now found around edges of cacao or coffee estates and—most importantly—in tropical, splashy-colored purple, crimson, orange and white Bougainvillaea vines.

Size and distribution make the Spurge family important, for over 23 genera grow in the West Indies. Of particular interest is the odd hanging red tassel Chenille plant and its cousin the red Beefsteak or Copper Leaf plant; the white Poinsettia, scarlet Fire Ball Poinsettia; vari-colored Crotons; Ricinus Castor-oil plant with striking foliage and lipstick-red pods; and various leafless Euphorbias.

The Periwinkle or Dogbane family offers velvety yellow Allamandas ("Cup of Gold") of two sizes; the fragrant and lovely Frangipani or Plumeria of showy, funnel-shaped waxy yellow, red or white blooms which were once used by Aztec Indians as religious offerings; Oleanders of yellow, pink and red are said to come from Asia or India but grow rampant here; fragrant Star Jasmine; the large delicate white cup flower, Beaumontia vine; and fragrant Carissa grandiflora or Natal Plum with its white blooms contrasted to red fruit and thorns. Today there is evidence that the little Periwinkle's root is a cancer cure.

Bignoniaceae reveals family secrets about its flowers in its name for they are usually big and showy. At least 18 genera of shrubs, vines and trees are found in this group in the Caribbean. Particularly lovely are the Purple Bignonia vine; canary yellow Cat's Claw Climber; Trumpet Creepers and Flame vines (Bignonia or Pyrostegia); red African Tulip trees (Spathodea); pink and golden Tabebuia or Tecoma and the rarest flower color—blue—found in masses of Jacaranda.

The Banana family accounted for early and continued economic progress in these islands. Its delicious yellow fruit is known around the world, while the beauty of its blossom cluster was known only to islanders. Lesser known plants but even more striking flowers are found on other members of this family.

The Bird of Paradise (Strelitzia reginae) originally from South Africa and named for a Queen is happy in the West Indies. Its unique flower suggests a golden-orange and blue crested bird's head and beak. It comes out on a long stalk looking like a stiff flag or bird's beak then breaks open and lifts its colorful crest more each day. There is also a White Bird of Paradise (Strelitzia nicolai). Another odd member of this family is the Traveler's Palm (Ravenala) of Madagascar. It is not a palm nor does it travel but it is said to grow only east and west in a flat arc which serves as a compass for lost travelers and yields a drinkable liquid.

Exotics of the Banana family are the Heliconias. Their dramatic inflorescences are made up of a stalk of alternating brilliant claw-shaped bracts. The entire inflorescence is usually hidden on the plant by large paddle-shaped leaves (the Golden Heliconia grows above its plant). The Lobster Claw Heliconia is as fire-red as a boiled lobster and the upright closed top bracts look like a lobster's claw with a darker color even outlining the design of one side clamped upon the other. Each claw may be 4 or 5 inches from stalk to tip while the arrangement of these claw-bracts can be 4 or 5 feet long. The Pink and Green Heliconia looks like the Lobster Claw but each bract has a pink boat-shaped center that blends down the side into yellow then into a green outline. The Hanging Heliconia is different. It has a long slender stem that sways the bracts like bunk-bed-cradles rocking the tiny flowers inside. Suddenly and dramatically, the stem droops and inverted red bracts sway from side to side. Heliconias were named for Mt. Helicon, home of Apollo and the Muses or goddesses of the arts and sciences.

Moving from these geometric design Heliconias, it's easy to place futuristic rocket blast-off-flame descriptions to another exotic family. The Ginger family (Zingiberaceae), botanically, is close to bananas and cannas in reed-type plants, blade-shaped leaves and some inflorescenses with colorful bracts enclosing small yellow-white flowers or large fragrant flowers that escape the bracts.

Torch Ginger (Phaeomeria magnifica) is one of the most spectacular flowers in the world. Tiny red bracts outlined in white are bunched up into a waxen cone-shaped torch on a long stalk growing straight up from the ground. This firey head has a collar of larger bracts and the entire torch is 9 or 10 inches across. The symmetrical cone grows and enlarges until the small true flowers push out from behind the overlapping bracts destroying the lines.

Red Ginger—often called Firey Feather or Hawaiian Ginger (Alpinia purpurata) has an upright inflorescence. Shell Ginger (Alpinia nutans) buds look exactly like a hanging string of white globe sea shells with the china-like pointed tips dipped in bright pink color. The buds open a few at a time as delicate white petals with red and yellow on them marked like some sea shells.

Spice Ginger or Candied Ginger (Chinese or Zingiber officinale) has a flower cluster or bracted spike of yellowish-green while the lip of the tiny flower is yellow-spotted purple. Ginger products are made from root stock.

White Ginger (Hedychium coronarium) looks like crystallized clouds of white butterflies and has a delightful fragrance. Against the dark green leaves and bulb-shaped stalk, these large flowers seem to wing their way out of a green cocoon. The Yellow Ginger is similar but even more delicate.

The Morning Glory family is combined with the Potato and Tomato families

(Continued on page 62)

FLAMBOYANT, ROYAL POINCIAN
(Delonix regia)

IXORA (*Ixora coccinea*)

SHRIMP PLANT
(*Beloperone
guttata*)

← CHENILLE
PLANT
(*Acalypha
hispida*)

→ BIRD OF
PARADISE
(*Strelitzia
reginae*)

44

ANDER
(*rium indicum*)

→
ANISH
YONET
(*cca aloifolia*)

47

I HAVE

↑
(Plumeria rubra)

FRANGIPANI, TEMPLE TREE

←
(Plumeria alba)

LOBSTER CLAW HELICONIA →
(Heliconia humilis)

AMANDA, GOLDEN BELL
(*amanda cathartica*)

BOUGAINVILLAEA
(*Bougainvillaea glabra*)

← PASSION
FLOWER
(*Passiflora
Caerulea*)

→ FLAME VIN
(*Pyrostegia
ignea*)

52

EEN OF THE NIGHT
(enicereus grandiflorus)

ORCHID TREE (Bauhinia variegata)

Description of foregoing pictures

FLAMBOYANT, ROYAL POINCIANA
(Delonix regia)
page 41

Igniting the skies with flames of red, this strikingly beautiful tree is considered a native of Madagascar but is equally at home in the West Indies. In fact, it was named for M. de Poinci, a governor of the French West Indies, and was growing wild in Jamaica in 1756. Its scarlet long-clawed-petal blossoms measure three to four inches across and are touched with yellow and white. They cover the wide-spreading limbs of trees which reach a height of sixty feet. The spectacular show of blooms also individually resemble orchids. These are followed by dangling pods often two feet long which are sometimes used as fuel in native fires ... and fuel for verbal battles when men, hearing the breeze-borne clatter of these pods, call the tree "women's tongues."

IXORA, FLAME OF THE WOODS,
JUNGLE GERANIUM (Ixora coccinea)
page 42

Rocket fire-balls or dense clusters of 1¼″ pin-wheel flowers with 4-5 lobes spreading out from long tubes make the Ixora a a most attractive evergreen shrub which may grow to small tree size. From the tropical East Indies but popular in the Caribbean, Bahamas, Bermuda and South Florida, this relative of the coffee family has almost the same glossy leaves whorled below the fireball or snowball head. Leaves contrast with flowers and the berry-like fruit. Ixora is named for a Malabar deity.

SHRIMP PLANT (Beloperone guttata)
page 43

Heart shaped rosy bracts overlap each other in scale fashion forming a curve with true flowers appearing from inside the tube near the tip end. Curved bracts and flowers together look so much like the curved tail of a shrimp that even highly scientific people are more likely to call this herbaceous little shrub by its common name. (Besides, Beloperone is a Greek allusion to the arrow-shaped anthers which aren't readily seen).

CHENILLE PLANT, RED HOT CAT-TAILS, MONKEY TAILS (Acalypha hispida)
page 44

Velvety tails of dark reddish-purple fur or chenille-like blooms may hang down as much as 18 inches from the green heart-shaped leaves. Tassels are made up of flowers without petals which are unbelievable until seen on these small bushes.

POINSETTIA, CHRISTMAS FLOWER
Euphorbia pulcherrima)

BIRD OF PARADISE, QUEEN'S FLOWER, BLUE TONGUE BIRD OF PARADISE (Strelitzia reginae)

page 45

A provocative and challenging exotic bird flower was first introduced from South Africa into England in the reign of George III and named after the Queen. Seeds of the first ones in the Caribbean may have hitch-hiked on slaves. Flowers are borne inside a pink or purplish-flushed sheath shaped like a bird's beak or the keel of a boat almost at right angles to the stem. Flowers spring out, usually one or two at a time, like the crest of a bird from its head or sails from a boat. Two brilliant orange (sometimes red) petaloid sepals pop out to stand upright flickering like flames. A third sepal lies flat until pushed up by the next opening flower. Petals are a deep blue with the stigma the javelin or arrow-like part of the flower. Usually tiny sun-birds pollinate the flowers.

OLEANDER, FLOWERING WIND-BREAK
(Nerium oleander, Nerium indicum)

page 46

Clusters of pink, rose, red, white and tones between bloom at the ends of branches of this tall shrub—usually 7-10 feet but may grow to 20 ft. tall branching at base—of the Periwinkle family. Some Oleander flowers are single with five lobes but most are double giving a fluted effect to 3″ width. Most are fragrant tho some botanists say only the N. indicum has perfume. Slender seed pods follow flowers. Slender leaves, in groups of three, are pointed and usually a dark dull green contrasting to lighter green on new growth. There is a rarer yellow Oleander. All parts of Oleanders are poisonous if eaten and smoke from burning bushes is also harmful.

SPANISH BAYONET, SPANISH DAGGER (Yucca aloifolia)

page 47

Semi-desert plants of the lily family, Yuccas are cultivated for their striking flower clusters. Common names come from sharp pointed leaves which are bayonet or dagger tip hard and sharp. Native uses for the plant are as needles and thread combined and for a liquid which ferments into a potent liquor. Their blossom cluster has been likened to a white lamp and white snow ball pile. These are native to the drier West Indian Islands.

FRANGIPANI, TEMPLE TREE
(Plumeria rubra and Plumeria alba)

page 48

Fragrance plus beauty caused this small tree to be a favorite for planting near temples and burying grounds . . . hence, its common name of Temple Tree. Centuries before white men found this tree, Aztec Indians used the flowers as religious rite offerings and anyone touching them or smelling them after the rites was put to death. The showy, funnel-shaped, fragrant blossoms of white, red or yellow were named after French Botanist Charles Plumier who made many voyages to the Caribbean in the 17th century. These trees are native to the West Indies and Tropical America but are found in both East and West Indies, Ceylon and Hawaii where blossoms are used for leis to adorn visitors' necks. Its fragrant waxy blossoms are seen on West Indian Islands. Many specific and varietal names have been given to the numerous color forms but are now regarded as one species—*P. rubra.* However, some garden lovers are continuing to call the white, *P. alba* or *P. acuminata* and the red, *P. rubra.*

LOBSTER CLAW HELICONIA
(*Heliconia humilis*)
page 49

Dramatic inflorescences are as red as boiled lobster and the hard bracts look like 4 or 5 inch open lobster claws piled upon each other. The true flowers are inside these hollow-curved bracts and are small green clusters that drown or rot when it rains so that each bract holds its own pool of water. Related to the banana, these are large paddle-shaped leaves which almost hide the striking bloom—and surely would were it not so brilliantly colored.

ALLAMANDA, GOLDEN BELL, GOLDEN TRUMPET (*Allamanda cathartica*)
page 50

Yellow Allamandas are popular vines which quickly cover fences, walls or buildings if tied up for they do not seem to cling as other vines. Because of this, they often remain as shrubs or clumps of glossy-green leaves perked up by profuse "solidified sunshine" in velvety yellow bells. Their buds are shades of chocolate and shiny—as if someone varnished each one.

BOUGAINVILLAEA, COLORED PAPER FLOWER (*Bougainvillaea glabra*)
page 51

This incredibly showy vine is probably the most widely planted ornamental vine of the tropics and a favorite in other southern areas. The vivid magentas, purples, reds and salmons you see are not real flowers but rather, comes from three bracts which surround tiny flowers. Texture of these bracts also gives them the name of "Paper Flowers." This vigorous thorny climber can be seen covering 70 foot trees or trained as hedges and shrubs. Their name comes from a French navigator, Louis de Bougainville, whose plant-hunting botanist brought specimens aboard in Rio de Janeiro in 1768 while supplies were being loaded. Bougainville was the first Frenchman to sail the Pacific on an expedition to the South Seas but his name is more remembered in this showpiece flowering vine of the tropics. It seems to bloom best in poor soil so even rocky mountain slopes and dry barren areas can support its color.

PASSION FLOWER, BLUE PASSION FLOWER, CRUCIFIXION STORY FLOWER (Passiflora caerulea)

page 52

Passion Flowers show the story of the Crucifixion in symbolism. Early explorers started the legends which continue today. First, the shades of purple have signified Christ's passion on the cross since earliest times. Purplish parts that flare into a many-pointed star always number 10—apostles at the Crucifixion (Judas and Peter absent). Centered is a sunburst of blue, white and purple filaments of the corona numbering 72 which ancient tradition says were the number of thorns in the Crown of Thorns. Five anthers symbolize the five wounds. Three

nails are there in the form of three styles with rounded stigmas. Cords and whips are seen in the coiling tendrils of the climbing vine; clutching hands of the persecutor-mob in the five lobed leaves. Lance-shaped leaves in some varieties symbolize Roman soldiers spears pierced into His side. Some have angel-wing leaves. Some have odd whitish spots on the underside which are likened to the 30 betrayal coins. On the back of flowers are three sepals symbolizing the Trinity. All but a few of the 300 species are native to the New World and many have edible fruits. Most popular for the fruit and a showier flower is P. quadrangularis or giant Granadilla from which jellies, jams, sherbets and delicate drinks are made.

FLAME VINE, ORANGE TRUMPET, TRUMPET CREEPER (Pyrostegia ignea or Bignonia venusta)

page 53

Sheets of flame cover trees, fences, walls and roofs when the Flame Vine is in bloom. The long slender red-orange tubes seem to be tongues of flame sweeping over the vine almost engulfing or hiding the green leaves and tendrils. Pyrostegia is Greek for fire and roof—roofs covered with this vine do seem to be on fire. Several varieties of these are native to the Caribbean and Brazil.

QUEEN OF THE NIGHT
(Selenicereus grandiflorus)
page 54

Queen of the Night is a good name for this large flower which could be said to resemble a crown but it's usually described as a many-petaled cup. White flowers, fragrant like vanilla, bloom at night and are up to 6 or 7″ in diameter with a scaly outside often with tufts of grey hair around the outer segments—salmon colored. It can be seen climbing or trailing from trees from the Caribbean area into the Bahamas, Florida and Bermuda. The fruit is berry-like but covered at first with bristles, hairs and spines. It is often confused with other night-blooming Cacti but the difference can be seen·in the ribbed or angled stems with small sparse spines. It is often called Hylocereus *(H. undatus, H. lemairei)* and Cereus grandiflorus but some of these are not fragrant. Selenicereus named for moon goddess and cereus.

ORCHID TREE, BAUHINIA, POOR MAN'S ORCHID *(Bauhinia variegata)*
page 55

Corsage orchids seem to grow on trees when these come into profuse bloom. In fact, when these blossoms are created into a corsage they truly become a "poor man's orchid." Twin lobed leaves gave this its name to commemorate the brothers Bauhin, 16th century herbalists. Native to India, this tree has "gone native" in the West Indies, growing wild since the early 1700's.

POINSETTIA, FIRE PLANT, PAINTED LEAF *(Poinsettia pulcherrima* or *Euphorbia pulcherrima)*
page 56

Yuletide symbol, these flaming beauties bloom over a six months' period in protected areas. Actually a shaggy head of leaves forms the red aureole or halo about its inconspicuous yellow flowers with the Ubangi lips in the center. This flower is termed a native of Mexico but has "gone native" in most of the Caribbean, Bahamas, Bermuda and in the U.S.A. from Key West to Charleston. The double red variety, *P. plenissima,* has larger blooms and lasts longer on the plant.

GERANIUM TREE OR CORDIA
(Cordia sebestena)
back cover

Flaming flower-clusters about six inches broad consist of a number of smaller individual blossoms as you can see here. Some flowers begin to appear in late spring but trees are usually at their best in June and July when laden with orange-scarlet flowers that are slightly crimped on their edges.

(Continued from Page 40)

(Solanaceae) and produces flowering vines of rich purple-blue, white, mauvish-pink, magenta, rose-purple or scarlet. These vines are found growing wild or cultivated in most of the islands.

The Coffee family (Rubiaceae) is important to the West Indies as a product but it also produces the highly popular Ixora shrubs. It is called Flame-of-the-Woods, Fire-Ball and Jungle Geranium for flame-reds and orange scarlets are the most commonly seen colors but there are yellow, pink and salmon Ixoras. They are seen as garden bushes or flowering hedges.

Family secrets of West Indian flowers could take a volume of books to discuss...a thousand pictures could not capture all their shades of shining colorful masses.

Tropical flowers are uniquely different. Individual flowers and unusual designs often catch the eye quicker than masses of color although tropics' colors are usually so vivid that a small plant or vine can create the same splash as a group of plants.

Most of the lovely West Indian flowers can be seen by normal sightseeing but many of the "unusuals" are only found in Botanical Gardens.

ISLAND BOTANICAL GARDENS OF TODAY

Recognizing flower lovers' and colonists' desires plus future economic progress problems, leading Governmental Botanists establish Botanical Gardens, Introduction and Experiment Stations today as they did in the past.

Botanical Gardens exist to introduce plants and flowers to the world—often improve varieties and hybrids. Directors and botanists assist local homeowners, city parks, colleges and commercial establishments to enhance their gardens. Oftentimes—because of this work—you may be able to see artistic displays, landscaping and even greater masses of flowers at hotel gardens and tourist attractions. But the newest or oldest and the most unusual plants are at the Botanical Gardens. Some have features in the West Indies you cannot see anyplace else in the world.

As you know, England's Royal Botanical Gardens at Kew was the Father of Horticultural Exchange. Her plant explorers and horticultural experts started founding Botanical Gardens in the Caribbean Islands over 200 years ago—which you can still visit today.

Outstanding are also the new Botanical Gardens in Freeport and Lucaya, Grand Bahama and some hotel gardens in Nassau, Bahamas. Most people do not knowingly travel for flowers, they see; but it's like a secret "siren song" drawing them unconsciously to beauty. So long as the West Indian Islands continue to blend excitement and comfort with natural floral beauty in their own unique way, they are destined to flower—in all senses of the word—as beautifully . . . perhaps more beautifully than any other place in the world.

Books by **HANS W. HANNAU,**

each one containing a collection of magnificent color photographs and a dramatic
description by this well-known photographer and writer.

The large volumes:

THE CARIBBEAN ISLANDS IN FULL COLOR
with 86 color pictures

THE BAHAMA ISLANDS IN FULL COLOR
with 66 color pictures

BERMUDA IN FULL COLOR
with 86 color pictures

U.S.A. IN FULL COLOR
with 176 color pictures

IN THE CORAL REEFS OF THE CARIBBEAN, BAHAMAS, FLORIDA AND BERMUDA
with 96 color pictures

The smaller popular editions:

ISLANDS OF THE CARIBBEAN
with 90 color pictures

ISLANDS OF THE BAHAMAS
with 68 color pictures

THE BERMUDA ISLES IN FULL COLOR
with 72 color pictures

BENEATH THE SEAS OF THE WEST INDIES
with 175 color pictures

TROPICAL FLOWERS
with 72 color pictures

THE ARGO BOOKS
with 45 color pictures

ELEUTHERA • ST. MAARTEN • JAMAICA
CURACAO • ARUBA • PUERTO RICO
ANTIGUA